GANESH

Remover of Obstacles

JAMES H. BAE

MANDALA

Contents

A God of Many Names

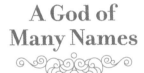

To those unfamiliar with the Vedic pantheon, its myriad gods and goddesses may appear startling or intriguing. One of the most cherished of all Hindu gods is Ganesh, and by his appearance, he may be considered the most enigmatic figure in the whole

pantheon. The image of Ganesh is replete with different meanings, and he is associated with numerous roles and cosmic functions. It is no surprise that even among Hindus, different understandings have evolved around his divine persona. In spite of that, he is one of the most dearly held and familiar figures in the life of the Hindu. Here are some of the roles he has assumed, in light of the scriptures and common understandings of his devotees.

Ganesh is the principal deity of beginnings. Hindus invoke his blessings for every passage in life: marriage, birth, business endeavors, and even before departing on a daily journey.

Ganesh, the remover of obstacles, is worshipped for the successful performance of one's duty in life, by which one attains perfection. He gifts his devoted followers with boons ranging from material prosperity to spiritual emancipation.

Ganapatyas (exclusive worshipers of Ganesh) regard him as the supreme god. He deters the activities of those with bad intentions, and to the sincere spiritual practitioner, he bestows his grace, by which they can move swiftly on a path of spiritual uplift.

Scriptural references regarding Lord Ganesh can be found in numerous Puranas, though the Ganesh Purana and Mudgala Purana deal exclusively with his worship and personal history. The earliest mention of Ganesh worship can be attributed to invocations found in the Rig Veda and Atharva Veda, where the name Ganapati is mentioned.

The names Ganesh and Ganapati translate as "Lord of Multitudes"

or "Lord of Hosts." As Lord of the Multitudes, he is seen as a universal benefactor and revered by Hindus for his merciful nature. When he is described as the Lord of Hosts, he is the general of Lord Shiva's army of demigods and attendants, which include the *maruts*, *vasus*, *rudras*, and many other groups of Vedic deities. In his work on Kundalini, Robert Svoboda suggests a deeper metaphysical meaning to the name Ganesh—"Lord of the Senses." The yogi who seeks freedom from the world approaches Ganesh for the ability to control his senses.

In many temples throughout India, Ganesh is incorporated into the worship of many other deities, such as Shiva, Vishnu, and the Goddess. His *murti*—deity form—or divine image is enshrined within their temple precincts, to be worshiped in the pilgrim's ritual act of entering the holy ground of the deity. Seated at gates and entrances, he is also known as the Lord of Thresholds, a guardian and keeper of sacred spaces.

Ganesh's Elephant Head

Several explanations are given as to how Ganesh acquired his elephant head. The best known account begins with Parvati, Lord Shiva's wife, bathing in a *kund* (lake) in Kailasa. After anointing her body with sandalwood paste, she removed a layer of it, from

which manifested a beautiful young child. The child, Ganesh, was employed to guard the entrance to the sacred pool and afford her privacy while she bathed, thus fulfilling his role as deity of thresholds.

Soon after, Lord Shiva returned and, upon seeing this unfamiliar child, he inquired who it was standing before him. Ganesh refused to allow Lord Shiva entrance, as he had been instructed by his mother. Mahadeva Shiva beheaded the child after a short struggle. Upon hearing of the incident, Parvati was displeased, and in order to appease her, Lord Shiva willed that the head of an elephant be joined to the child's body. With his elephant-headed form, Lord Ganesh was from here on out recognized as the divine child of Shiva and Parvati and the sibling of Skanda.

Scholar and devotee of Ganesh John A. Grimes describes Ganesh's decapitation as referring to the transformation we must undergo in order to attain spiritual awakening. The loss of the head is a metaphor for transcendence of the ego,

by which we live in the infinite freedom of nondual consciousness. Another account has Ganesh appearing in Lenyadri, the mystical cave where he spent his first fifteen years. In this history, Parvati apparently gave birth to him after performing intense austerities for a period of twelve years. From a metaphysical perspective, Ganesh appearing in the cave signifies his appearance in the human heart, illuminating the mind of the fettered soul and awakening divine cognizance. Other sources relate that he was self-born, or manifested from the divine aura of Shiva. The variations in details are a common feature in Vedic literature; the sages are known to speak of different incarnations in different eras, making it difficult to distinguish one appearance of Ganesh from another.

When the revelation of the Mahabharata entered the heart of the great sage Badarayan Vyasa, he called upon Sri Ganesh to record its contents. Such a complex transmission of oral teachings would require the subtlest intelligence and sharpest memory

to record. Thus, Ganesh agreed
to perform this service under the
condition that Vyasa would narrate
the epic in one continuous sitting,
without a pause in the dictation.
Vyasa agreed, posing the condition
to Ganesh that he would have to
give himself completely to the oral
transmission, realize its essence,
and thus be able to communicate its
deep message in a way accessible to
all classes of human society. Ganesh
then removed one of his tusks
and used it to record the entire
Mahabharata as Vyasa spoke.

From this event, we have an

explanation of Ganesh's appearance
as the elephant-headed god bearing
a single tusk—called Ekadanta, or
"bearing one tusk." Ganesh was
from then on recognized as the
divine scribe. The Mudgala Purana
says, "the word 'one' is the symbol of
illusion (*maya*); from it everything
has sprung. The tooth (or tusk)
is the support of existence; it is
therefore the impeller of illusion.

Lord of
Wisdom

Ganesh, in Vedic spirituality, is a deity presiding over knowledge. He is shown in an image with the goddess Saraswati, who presides over knowledge, both material and spiritual. She is often represented with a vina, a divine musical instrument, by

which she enlightens living beings with the inner meaning of the Vedas. Dennis Hudson's essay "The Ritual Worship of Devi" describes the function of goddess Saraswati: "The sacred knowledge revealed by Saraswati through the mantras of Veda includes ritual and music, and Saraswati is therefore the mother of priests and musicians when they function as such; she is believed to sit on their tongues to guide them . . . "

In India, many scholars and spiritual practitioners perform austerities on the occasion of

Saraswati Puja, to obtain a blessing of higher learning. Similarly, Ganesh is invoked by jyotishis (Vedic astrologers); as a deity of astrology, he knows the destinies of all living beings. Ganapatyas and Shaivites regard him as an overseer of intricate karmas, based on our previous actions. In the Gayatri Tantra, Ganesh is said to have inscribed the Tantras as Lord Shiva dictated them to him, thus indicating his intimate knowledge of esoteric spiritual matters.

Symbol and Reality

"**P**ictures invite the eye not to rush along, but to rest a while and dwell with them in enjoyment of their revelation." Divine symbols have the power to impart insight and inner vision of the reality they represent. The symbol contains the very essence of the reality behind it;

in this way, it is just as much a living reality as it is a representation. Symbol and reality are a unity that transcends mundane distinctions. Spirit enters the phenomenal world and remains revealed in art, the sacred literatures, and the mantras of the Vedas.

To Hindus, the divine image (murti) worshiped in homes and in temples is a visible expression of the Deity whose spiritual nature transcends mundane perception. Hindus approach divinity through these forms, recognizing their encounters as a valid experience of the unlimited, an undeniable contact with the reality that underlies the image. Inherent in the form and structure of the divine image is the power that beckons us to change, as the truth of its reality pierces through the veil of our historical mind.

Passages from the Mugdala Purana narrate several accounts surrounding Ganesh's advent in different eras and forms. These histories give the scriptural context surrounding different iconographic representations, such as his riding the mouse, appearing in a four-

॥ श्री गणेशाय नमः ॥

armed form, or upholding a mouse banner, with a potbelly or twisted trunk. Each points out his advent for the purpose of defeating a different demonic personality at a different time in history.

In this regard, John A. Grimes lists sixteen features employed in many classical Ganesh murtis: elephant face (*gajamukha*); twisted trunk (*vakratunda*); protruding belly (*lambodara*); dwarfish stature (*kharva*); or having very short legs (*padambujahyam ativamanabhyam*); odd appearance (*vikata*); fanlike ears (*supakarna*);

small eyes (*hrasvanetra*); long trunk (*lambanasa*); black tusks (*syamadanta*); ash gray color (*dhumravarna*), naked or clad in the skin of a tiger (*digambara*, *vyaghracarma*); bald head (*khalvata*); fond of eating (*carvanalalasa*); hidden ankles (*gudhagulpha*); carrying a waterpot (*kamandaludhara*); and mouse as a mount or vehicle (*akhuketana*). Ganesh is generally represented with one tusk and tooth. Elephant headed, with a humanlike or celestial form, his appearance is deeply suffused with metaphysical symbolism. The elephant is a symbol of the virtue and wisdom that Ganesh embodies. He is often seen riding a mouse, showing how the mischievous nature of the ego can be conquered by the vast, awakened nature of spiritual consciousness. Another beautiful interpretation is to see the weight of Ganesh as symbolizing divine grace, the mouse being the human soul receiving and acting as a vehicle of this mercy. His very body seems a paradox, a combination of human and divine elements that show him to be radically free and unconditioned and, simultaneously, in touch with nature and the world.

Known as *Lambodara*, Ganesh has a potbelly and is fond of sweets—especially the *modhak*, or sweet ball offered by his devotees. Ganesh is often depicted wearing the *svastika*, which Alain Daniélou describes as "the graphic symbol of Ganesh. It is made of a cross representing the development of the multiple from the basic unity, the central point, but each of its branches is bent so that it does not aim toward the center. This is intended to show that we cannot reach the basic unity directly through the outward forms of the universe. Hence the way toward principle (*tattva*) is said to be crooked."

Some sects regard the modhak as a symbol for *maha-buddhi*, or supreme wisdom; others see in it a representative of the seed of creation. In the vast expanse of being, represented by Ganesh's round belly, all living beings reside.

Worship of Ganesh

Ganesh worship appears late in the evolution of the Vedic pantheon, yet he is prominent in contemporary times. In the course of time, his influence extended to Nepal, Tibet, and even as far east as China, where he holds a mostly peripheral position relative to

Buddhist and Tantric thought. In certain instances, the worship of Ganesh has taken a more central role in esoteric forms of Chinese Buddhism. Orthodox ritualists of the Puranic tradition worship the five central deities of the Hindus, known as *Panchopasana*: Ganesh is accompanied by Surya, Shiva, Durga, and Vishnu in many temples throughout India.

The central place of worship of the Ganapatyas is found at Margoan. Here, *Mayuresvara* (Ganesh) is worshiped along with his eight other primary avatars. According to the Mugdala Purana, this temple is the primary seat of worship on Earth. The eight deities alongside Mayuresvara are Ekadanta, Vikata Mahodara, Gajanana, Lambodara, Vighnaraja, Dhumravarna, and Vakratunda. All are surrounded by accounts narrated in scriptures, such as the Mugdala Purana.

Lord Ganesh's worship is predominant in Tamil Nadu and Maharashtra, where many temples house his holy image. In Mumbai and throughout Maharashtra, devotees worship him each year for ten days leading up to Ganesh

Chaturthi, when a large murti of him is ritually brought to a local waterway, accompanied by an elaborate procession. From there, thousands of joyous supplicants dance, celebrate, and offer prayers as Ganesh disappears into the body of water and moves beyond the world of the senses. This holy festival is also observed by Hindus worldwide as they invite his divine presence into their homes; clay forms of Ganesh are worshiped and then brought to the ocean or another body of water to be dissolved, thus enacting this divine *lila*.

One might relate this ritual cycle to the Hindu and Buddhist concept of *maya*: that all life is illusory by its ephemeral nature. Art, which is an interpretation of life, can be valid a vehicle for deeper, fundamental experiences. Indeed, the art of painting, by its very nature as a temporary creation, is powerful in its symbolic language. Ritual art exposes the ephemeral nature of material phenomena while also suffusing and embodying eternal, spiritual reality through its symbolic progression. Thus the ritual is served through forms, images, scents, sounds, and the exchange of the real in the perceptive heart of the audience as it journeys through its cycle, to close and leave us again longing for union with the divine.

Wendy Doniger O'Flaherty discusses the ritual cycle: "There are other reasons for this emphasis on impermanence. The material traces of a powerful ritual must vanish in order that the power not remain causally at hand when the ritual awareness of it has ended. In Benares, life-sized clay images of Rama and Sita are made for the

Ramlila festivals and then thrown away; the same is true of the images of Ganesh used in ceremonies in Maharashtra. For the festival of Durga Puja in Bengal, hundreds of more-than-life-sized statues of the goddess Durga are made and beautifully decorated; at the end of the celebration, the statues are carried down to the Ganges in torchlight parades at night and cast into the dark waters."

In yogic and Tantric thought, Ganesh is connected with the principle of prana, or mobility. He is also regarded as the master of sound, embodiment of the sacred syllable *Om*, and approachable by sacred mantras related to the names of his numerous divine manifestations. At the base of the spine, Ganesh is said to preside over the *muladhara chakra*, the base psychophysical center pertaining to the element earth. It is here that the goddess Kundalini is said to reside in dormancy, and can be awakened through the power of Ganesh.

Some sources regard Ganesh as a celibate and the shelter of brahmacharins; others portray him as wedded to his consorts

Siddhi and Buddhi. Later *Shakta* (goddess cults) developments include the worship of Ganesh with a consort. Another form of worship by groups of Ganapatyas centered around five esoteric forms of Ganesh accompanied by a feminine counterpart, recognized as aspects of Shakti-Ganapati.

Ganesh, as Lord of Thresholds, represents the face of change that dawns at every new situation we confront in life. He stands at the gateway of perception. His figure symbolizes a seizure of the old, a separation from the

dead perception of the solid,
banal details of daily events, and
a new life to be lived. The image
of his immense form riding the
mouse challenges us to accept our
situation, bear the weight of our
reality, and transcend; otherwise,
we find ourselves living out a sense
of burden.

Choice is an inseparable part
of life. Our options in life appear
rigid and ordained at times, but
in truth it is the dichotomies of
consciousness that fix them and
limit our perception of possibility.
Ganesh opens us up to the vital,

intuitive mind. This expansive point of departure allows us to face change, make progressive choices, and better understand destiny. With a broader, deeper perspective, we can approach circumstances as they appear in our lives. As we embrace this stage more fully, it may seem as if the same basic lessons and figures emerge to be confronted over and over. But ever greater clarity, depth, and significance are revealed to us by those forms. And now Ganesh, the face of change, appears everpresent.

The Iconography of the Ganesh Image

Ganesh's form is humanlike, with a round, protruding belly. He has the head of an elephant, his mount is the mouse, and he is commonly seen with four hands holding modhak, noose, and goad (pointed rod). What do all these symbolize? What can the depictions

श्रीगजानन विना एक गणेशजी

mean to one devoted to Ganesh, and wishing to learn from him?

His elephant head atop his humanlike form represent harmony of Spirit and Nature; the infinite and finite alike are integrated in his divine persona.

His large head is a sign of intellect and a call to think bigger, while his fanlike ears indicate wisdom and the ability to listen to those who call for help, and urge the viewer to listen closer and learn ever more. His trunk is a symbol of discrimination, the ability to determine good from evil.

The roundness of creation is situated in the expanse of his form. The entirety of the cosmos can be contained in his belly, the shape of which also encourages us to peacefully take in all our experiences, whether good or bad.

An image of Ganesh with only two arms is considered taboo and inappropriate to the deity; he is depicted with at least four arms to represent intellect (*buddhi*), ego (*ahamkara*), mind (*manas*), and conditioned conscience (*chitta*). All of those arms are controlled by Ganesh, who himself symbolizes

pure conscious awareness (atman), which unites all those aspects to work together.

Depicted at times either standing with one leg raised and the other lowered, or seated with legs crossed and one foot reaching to the ground, Ganesh's posture is a symbol that encourages us to exist in and experience both the material and spiritual worlds.

Ganesh is often seen holding a modhak, representing the seed of creation as well as the individual soul. The noose and the goad symbolize hindrance toward unrighteous activity and encouragement toward the path of virtue and upliftment. Along with these items, he sometimes bears a lotus flower (*padma*) in one hand, as a symbol of the highest reaches of human enlightenment of the spirit; in other images he holds a trident (*trishula*), the weapon of Shiva, as a symbol of time and Ganesh's own mastery of it. In many depictions, one hand is empty, turned toward the viewer in a gesture (*mudra*) for protection and blessing (*abhaya*).

The mouse, a symbol of ego and craftiness, is ridden by Ganesh as

a vehicle or mount; without similar control over our desires and our ego, they can end up taking us for a ride instead.

Overall, by his many depictions, Ganesh teaches humanity about choice and progression, and his jolly temperament reveals his love and compassion.

The God of Beginnings

Among his many titles, Ganesh is called the God of Beginnings, for it is at the beginning of a journey, venture, or life change—however great or small—that his guidance and protection is sought. As spiritual beings on a human journey, we

share a desire for a common goal. We seek to be fulfilled. We seek to be enlightened. And, while we are fellow seekers, each one of us follows a unique path. We each arrive at fulfillment by different means and under vastly different conditions. In honoring our uniqueness and the path that is ours alone to take, we find solace. For countless ages, individuals have sought to answer the enduring question of how to achieve lasting happiness. It is our very nature to desire happiness, the possibility of which is locked within the prison of our human design, chained to the everyday functions of our body, mind, and heart. Our purpose, then, is to explore how this potential for happiness is confined, in order to know how it can be freed. Underlying our existence is a deep intelligence that communicates itself through the dialogue of the "ordinary" events that shape our lives. From this perspective, nothing is accidental, and our notion of the triviality of daily experience is transcended. Traditional wisdom teaches us that when we participate in this dialogue, we will not only be fulfilled and able to enjoy the sense of well-being that comes with such fulfillment, but we will contribute to the well-being of others as well. This is so because following one's true path begins with the realization that one's whole being is deeply connected to all of life.

Ganesh in Mythology

Symbolism abounds in the sacred mythology of our wisdom traditions. Mythology acts as a guide in which to navigate the symbols, or signals, which appear in our everyday lives. The paradox we live with, of course, is that while the fundamental lessons from which we

seek to learn present themselves as tangible life situations, we often fail to recognize or engage them in truly instructional ways because of our own habits and misconceptions. The understanding we desire is within us, but we must first learn to see—something mythology can help teach us.

Ganesh appears in many forms, signifying the diversity of human destiny. In South Indian traditions, he is unmarried and fully devoted to his mother, Parvati. In the North, Ganesh is a householder with two consorts,

Siddhi and Buddhi, known as Achievement and Wisdom, respectively. As Bala Ganesh, the divine child, he is curious and full of folly. He is playful and loving, though he understands deeply the predicament of others. The modhak, or sweet confection, he accepts from his beloved devotees represents not only his innocence but of his pearls of wisdom. As the dancing god, Ganesh balances out the severity of every step we take, inspiring realization of the divine behind all of life's circumstances, and the joy of living life in concert

with the whole. In other forms, Ganesh embodies wisdom and judgment. He is the force of change. In still others, he is the overseer of karma.

Ganesh reigns over both the divine and the demonic, and everywhere in between. His powers affect both gods and demons alike, as well as each of us. A paragon of "this-worldliness" and "other-worldliness," Ganesh moves easily and enigmatically between many worlds. Not only is he emblematic of a truth that is all-encompassing, he honors our humanity—our hopes, ideals, and aspirations—as well as our spirituality. Ganesh teaches us what it is to be truly human. He shows us that living demands a dynamic search for truth, a daring move from familiar, sometimes dangerous, habits and perceptions to a more spontaneous and sincere path to the Divine.

Remover of
Obstacles

For Hindus, and many Jains and Buddhists, Ganesh is known as Vighneshvar, Remover of Obstacles. He is worshipped for protection during journeys, successful performance of tasks, benedictions in business matters, and many other basic concerns. Appealing to

Ganesh assures a smooth path. He offers gifts of health and prosperity, connecting one with creation's abundance, and inspires us to understand the deep connection between our worldly experience and the spiritual. Ganesh has not only the power to remove obstacles but also to place them so we might learn a much-needed lesson or two. What may initially appear as an obstacle can ultimately be seen as a source of strength and a tool for self-exploration and understanding. Ganesh confronts us through the mask of our challenging life circumstances, so that we may move about conscientiously and with honest intentions. In our daily lives, we work to balance all of the elements that are important to us: personal time, work, creativity, family, relationships, and spiritual practice.

These basic priorities afford us the chance to find joy and meaning, as well as meet our practical needs. But it is not easy to find balance: Not everything goes as planned. Obstacles often challenge us, and it takes perseverance and clarity for us to meet our needs. But success

is not simply about achieving our endeavors or the desired result of our actions. We must recognize unexpected openings, or opportunities, in obstacles. One believes that there is only destiny, and another, that magic and infinite possibility are in every situation. One belief without the other is incomplete—to overcome personal obstacles, we must recognize that both possibilities exist, and that life is ultimately full of grace.

Lord of
Thresholds

Ganesh is also known as the Lord of Thresholds. In India, his statues are placed at the inner gates of many temples, symbolizing the role as keeper of sacred spaces. Pilgrims and passersby pay homage and seek his blessings. It is this symbolic presence at the entrances

of holy places that makes Ganesh so vital in our lives. At a threshold, between the possibility of the profound and our often habitual perception of the world, Ganesh is behind the moment of experience where human desire and possibility meet. He stands at the threshold of old and new, sacred and profane, the wisdom of old religious and social practices and the complex modern age we live in. He connects *dharma*, a truthful way of living, from the distant past to the present.

The Bridge
of Dharma

Dharma addresses our sense of separation from the Absolute, the search for personal fulfillment, collective well-being, and adapting inherited wisdom and values to the present. Dharma is the essence of life, bringing all beings and things together in harmony. In contrast

to dharma is our infatuation with individual experience, singular fulfillment, and pleasure. The cause of suffering and despair is narcissism—our sense of separateness. It is not desire for pleasure that causes dissatisfaction, but disconnection with the spiritual, as a result of putting so much potential for our happiness in the pursuit of material pleasure, which is only misery masked as temporary fulfillment. We are fulfilled when we discover the reason for our creation and live truthfully. But our happiness depends not solely on being personally fulfilled but also on contributing to the fulfillment of others. The gift of our uniqueness is not for us alone: it is given so that we may share it with family, community, and God. Dharma is a universal principle that engages us through our experiences so that we progress. Life reveals dharmic insights into how best to live with integrity. The deeper we explore this concept, the closer we are to freeing ourselves from the constraints of personal desire.

Blessings
from Ganesh

Two objects often associated with Ganesh are his noose and his goad. As symbols, these objects represent a life that is both individually nourishing and universally sustaining, or balanced. The noose is a fear-inducing icon, one that is meant to deter

individuals from performing acts that are harmful to themselves or others. When we try to assert ourselves in detrimental ways, life seems to pull the reins. Even when we think we have positive intentions, we might not necessarily see the whole picture. Ganesh's noose reminds us that we need to slow down and examine our intentions, in order to ensure that they are honest. Otherwise, we might find ourselves in uncomfortable, even threatening positions. Similarly, Ganesh's goad encourages us in dharmic ways. The sharp goad represents the narrow and often challenging obstacle-strewn path one must walk. It is also said to represent protection. Ganesh protects us and opens doors in our lives so that we can proceed with confidence. When nothing stands in the way of our efforts, or when we arrive safely, we can perceive it as a blessing from Ganesh.

The Play of
the Divine

Once, Ganesh was riding on his vehicle, the mouse, and ravenously consuming handfuls of his dessert of choice, modhak—a sweet confection made of milk, flour, and sugar. Suddenly, a snake crossed his path. Naturally, the mouse shrieked and reared back

out of fear, and the great Ganesh fell
onto the ground, belly first. Upon
impact, his rotund belly exploded,
and all of the sweets he had eaten
poured out in every direction.
Upset, Ganesh grabbed the snake
and tied his belly back together
with it. Meanwhile, up above, the
moon laughed at the whole event.
So, Ganesh pulled out one of his
tusks and threw it at the Moon, and
darkness fell upon the Earth. Later
the Moon was restored, but because
of the damage wrought by the tusk,
it was never whole again. That is why
the Moon appears to wax and wane.

Using iconography and imagery associated with Ganesh, this myth explains the phenomenon of the lunar cycle. In traditional contexts, narratives that surround the gods, such as this one, are called lila, or "the play of the divine." Lila narratives portray the folly of the gods in contrast to the actual power, freedom, and grace the gods more often exhibit. From outside of tradition, the myths that surround different deities are but stories told to communicate universal themes. Within the tradition, differing views are only reconciled by devotion and personal experience of the divinity of the deity; otherwise, details remain a mere mystery. Ganesh's anger in this scenario shows just how caught up in our emotions we can get, and, in turn, how defensive we can act, especially when we find ourselves at the center of criticism or ridicule. Such a response reveals how strongly we are attached to our self-image and just how far we will go to restore and maintain that self-image. Attachment to our emotions can make us cling to the outer appearance of things and take us away from the truth.

Beyond emotion, there is reason. Reason allows us to take inventory of our personal reality. With reason we understand our emotions—the emotions that detract from our full involvement in life.

But reason can become a problem when we try to rationalize our negative behavior or interpret it in self-centered ways. The overly rational person will evade the truth of the matter by creating a pretty myth, an elaborate self-image, wherein trials become melodramas and trivialities evolve into spectacles that others are

forced to admire. Reason and intellect should be tools for honesty and introspection, rather than for dressing up our circumstances.

Our emotional and rational selves are deeply connected with our human instincts, and govern basic aspects of human experience. A functional harmony is needed between the two. We lose something of our humanity when we do not address each part of our self. The road to fulfillment requires balance. The play between emotion, reason, and instinct connects us to the outside world, and the more we integrate them, the more we gain. These elements of human personality are but reflections of our soul's inherent nature, which, in an integrated and evolved state, expresses universal values of wisdom, compassion, truthfulness, and loving. The human personality must be fine-tuned and integrated into the work of the soul. The approaches and attitudes toward such work are reflected in the interpretations of Ganesh mythologies, which illustrate how to purposefully integrate our feeling, thinking, and instinct into our lives.

Each of our lives is unique in its design. Each of us has a unique purpose in this lifetime. The lessons we need to learn are embedded deep within us, and demand an unfolding or widening of our sense of self. But that sense is subtle and complex. Uncovering our deepest self from the layers of self-image is an arduous task. Fulfillment can only occur when we are alive to our highest potential, to a sense of self beyond our many roles and sides. This is the part of us that survives all the struggles and predicaments that we face. It

has taken us through the gateway of birth and remains beyond the frontier of death. This self is joyous and radiant. It never wrestles with dissatisfaction, and is the deepest basis of our personhood and presence. Knowing this self is to be enlightened.

We begin to sense this deepest self as the very thread of continuity that underlies our daily experience. What changes is merely our external identity and behavior, both of which are influenced by our humanity. The balance of emotion, reason and instinct that we maintain in our personal lives affects our self-understanding. The following narrative reveals much about how we function in both freedom and bondage, and about the play of feeling, rationality, and passion.

The Divine Child

According to Hindu lore, Ganesh is the son of Parvati, goddess of creation and wife of Lord Shiva, the god of destruction. The tale of Ganesh's birth and how he came to have an elephant's head reveals the necessity of an open-minded attitude in the face of obstacles.

In the story, Parvati was bathing in her private sanctuary. Shiva had ventured off to perform austerities. Feeling lonely, longing for a child, Parvati yearned for the company and affection of a son. Mimicking the manner of the world's creation, she shaped a beautiful boy from an earthen mixture and brought him to life. Parvati loved the child and was no longer alone. He guarded the entrance of her private bath to ward off any intruders.

When Shiva returned home, he found a stranger at Parvati's door. Obeying his mother's orders, the child refused entry to the mighty god. Vexed, Shiva unleashed his fury and the boy's head fell from his body.

Upon seeing what had happened to her beloved child, Parvati grieved and would not leave her sanctuary until Shiva replaced the head of her beautiful boy. Shiva's attendants went in search of the first being they saw, to be sacrificed so that he could keep his promise. The first being they found was an elephant. Soon after, the child was restored to life with the elephant's head. He became known as Gajanana, or Ganesh, "The Elephant-Headed One."

Just as there are many ways to interpret mythology, there are infinite ways to perceive any given situation. A single event can cause a spectrum of feelings in as many people. We must learn to examine just how settled we are in the ways that we view things. Without a desire to see more deeply, we remain closed to the depth of life's events and live only on the surface, within the limited sphere of our projections. Ganesh's beginnings also teach us that every spiritual transformation requires a profound turn within. His decapitation symbolizes a freedom from ego, a retreat into a space of unknowing. In our lives, we are vulnerable to challenging experiences, just as Parvati's child was vulnerable to Shiva's wrath. Such experiences as illness, life changes, and the loss of loved ones allow us to see that our only way out is to move within, and to confront tragedy and uncertainty with our own inner stability. This inward focus allows us to see that our many experiences unite with the will of God.

Boundaries

In the story of Ganesh's mystical birth, he is stationed as a keeper at the door of his mother's sanctuary. His duty is to protect her from intruders. As the Lord of Thresholds, Ganesh reminds us about the importance of guarding our space and setting

boundaries. Boundaries are not necessarily limitations. They can be practical guidelines we uphold for functionality. We set boundaries to ensure that we give ourselves the space we need to develop our inner lives and to live with integrity. Throughout our lives, from childhood to adulthood to old age, we constantly reshape the boundaries of our identity. As our lives change and we develop as individuals, old boundaries dissolve and new ones form. Life circumstances keep changing, and hopefully, we keep evolving.

Boundaries lose their efficacy when we regard them as absolutes. At some point, we let go of boundaries. We learn to define ourselves and our beliefs beyond the bounds of dogmas and social norms. In the face of truth, our boundaries collapse. Ganesh reveals to us that eventually, we have to let down our guard and remain sensitive to the messages at hand.

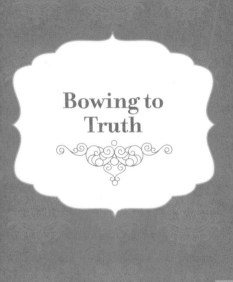

Bowing to Truth

Ganesh is also known as Ekadanta because he is depicted as having one tusk. Some scriptures say Ganesh lost his tusk in battle with a great warrior sage named Parashuram. According to ancient Vedic record, Parashuram, regarded as an avatar of Vishnu,

singlehandedly defeated a ruling
warrior class and reestablished
religion according to true Vedic
principles, as it had been corrupted
over time. In the story of his
battle with Ganesh, Parashuram
represents the face of truth and
Ganesh represents the wisdom of
bowing to truth.

Parashuram wished to pay
homage to Shiva at his holy abode
of Kailash. There at the entrance,
he met Ganesh, who was positioned
so that no one would disturb his
father. Parashuram was not inclined
to listen to this mere child and

proceeded eagerly to see Shiva. Ganesh stood his ground and would not allow the great sage to enter.

A fierce battle ensued between the two. Finally, Parashuram wielded his famed axe and hurled it at his opponent. When Ganesh saw this amazing weapon, he recognized it as a sign from Shiva—the weapon was originally Shiva's own—and bowed to it, in the direction of grace. The axe struck Ganesh, breaking his tusk, and he allowed Parashuram to enter.

When we are dedicated to truth and living with integrity, sometimes

we know to "bow" in circumstances others might see as our time of gain. We bow because in this moment we sense our highest purpose, and we understand that the real gain is, and can only be, an internal one.

Outwardly, we may at times step away or retreat from relative success. Some scriptures say that Ganesh was beginning to get the upper hand in his battle with Parashuram. In this encounter, Ganesh teaches us to seek the essence in any situation. In our lives, this sense of choosing to follow what is essential may take the form of not accepting a job offer that might bring monetary gain, but in the long run would detract time from a rewarding personal relationship or spiritual practice. It could also mean not needing to insist on being acknowledged as "right" in an argument even when one might, in fact, be correct, or not accepting undue praise.

Bowing to truth also means understanding that truth is everpresent and in unlimited forms in order to engage and teach us. The story of Ganesh bowing to his opponent inspires the act of

"seeing" the hand of God in the ordinary events of our daily lives.

Ganesh's single tusk signifies a realization that there is an essential unity or connectedness in all things. Revelation is not bound only to sacred words scripted on palm leaves but can also be seen in and as the world in every moment. We can engage in life in this way when we have established contentment and acceptance in our hearts.

इन्द्र शर्मा

The Way of Wisdom

There is no adequate map of the terrain of personal growth, but there are universal roads that individuals have traveled to achieve happiness. The story of Ganesh and Skanda weaves together some basic themes of aspiration and journey in a number of teaching tales.

Once, Ganesh and Skanda had a friendly dispute over who should be considered senior among the two divine siblings, and decided on a race: Whoever could circle the universe and return first would receive the position. Skanda quickly mounted his peacock and raced off, leaving Ganesh in his wake.

His own companion, the mouse, was no challenge to his brother's mount, but Ganesh was undeterred. Silently, he folded his hands in prayer, then slowly and reverently circumambulated his parents, Shiva and Parvati, bowing his head when done. When asked about the meaning of his action, Ganesh stated that one's parents are the center of the universe and that by circumambulating them, he had made a full passage. Pleased by his devotion, Shiva and Parvati declared him the senior.

This tale illustrates the power of devotion and dedication in overcoming challenges in life. From a spiritual perspective, there are two paths to development: the way of wisdom, and of love or devotion.

The way of wisdom involves discerning between truth and

falsehood, and applying that knowledge. The way of devotion entails self-surrender to God: a path of humility, service, and joy.

Either way is a genuine path to overcoming obstacles and articulates the approaches to achieving lasting fulfillment—that of effort and of grace. In either case, the spiritual path requires skill, sensitivity, and discretion in action. Our actions and intentions bring us either limitation or freedom, depending on how we choose to act.

Just like the young, robust Skanda, we may see a in ourselves a certain tendency to get caught up in the lure of outward success. Skanda reveals to us the need to be able to actualize our goals with dedication and perseverance. We must bridge personal conviction by practical and pragmatic service. The treasure of our true self is beyond the grasp of any narcissistic concern. Ganesh signals us to be clear and responsive to our heart's call and honor the duties we are granted.

The Spirit of the Journey

The demands of everyday life are endless. Obligations and desires can preoccupy us and keep us from fully living. But then, the life we live can be dynamic and creative if we don't let obstacles block the flow of our conscious existence, hiding the truth in daily life.

Our work in life involves first developing a healthy sense of personhood, and then transcending and integrating it. Along the way, traumas or conflicts condition us and challenge our growth. Much of our time is spent just maintaining our emotional lives and physical conditions. To move ahead, we often have to clear the trail as we go. Progress and development do not occur without change in our motivations and actions.

One of many symbols that adorn the images of Ganesh is the svastika, which represents the dynamic unity of all things with their source. Each spoke or branch of the svastika has vertical and horizontal lines, symbolizing our individual paths to fulfillment that are crooked like the movement of a snake or a winding trail through the forest. Our commitment to truth must be one of radical honesty and, consequently, flexibility.

Each bend of our life's course embodies a natural harmony—one that is both guided and created by each step we take. At every juncture, at every moment, the situations we face fit the design of our life course.

They are orchestrated to help us develop our human potential and, if we recognize their inherent value, they facilitate positive movements in our personal progression. The winding paths that we traverse involve both a degree of personal determination to find fulfillment, and a sense of willingness to let our lives unfold as they may. In any of these movements, we must remain loyal to our hearts. Otherwise, we act not out of love and care, but out of denial, repression, or rationalization of unprogressive attitudes. The measure of progress is to leave behind the old and embrace new growth and development.

Over and over again we come to crossroads in our lives—critical junctions where we are forced to take leaps of faith to regain what is essential. As Guardian of Thresholds, Ganesh teaches us that these junctures are the times to jump, to make decisions and embrace any changes that are necessary to move forward. The choices we make at these moments largely determine the course of our personal development and the

circumstances that lie ahead of us. Every stage of our lives comes to a natural end. Our work and our relationships, which largely define our sense of identity, are pervaded with a sense of finality. At some point, an inner shift occurs when all of these chapters of our lives hold no meaning for us and we are called to address higher pursuits.

Life in
the Real

The distinction between worldly and spiritual life is nebulous—the spiritual and the material are inextricably bound. The life we live either reflects this essential harmony or is wrought with seeming contradictions and challenges that call for this

realization. Ganesh reconnects us with the present moment of experience wherein we realize its connection to the Divine. Our life pathway is one of innocence, of listening, and of accepting the circumstances dealt to us. Personal freedom is met through challenging ordeals, the purpose of which is to skillfully liberate us from the grips of ego that binds us. Life is sacred. Our deeds should embrace this noblest of truths. Ganesh—in all his forms—impresses upon us the idea of an honest and complete human life. He is at the heart of an evolving

mythology, whose interpretation and inspiration yield instruction for living a practical life. Embodied within this wisdom is a spiritual impetus that compels us to live the truth sought in all ages by all peopl' of free will and heart.

Aware of the passions that uphold the human spirit and the truth that brings relevance and harmony, Ganesh offers a beginning, a path of faith—a positive and intentional approach to living. It is a path that moves in spontaneity: beyond form and formlessness, beyond personality

and impersonality, and beyond dogma and disobedience. It is neither the ascetic path nor that of the aesthete. It is an inner following and an honest joyfulness, an undefined way of the heart flowing from the depth of Being.

BIBLIOGRAPHY

Campbell, Joseph. *The Mythic Image.*
Princeton, NJ: Princeton University P., 1981.

Daniélou, Alain. *The Hindu Temple:
Deification of Eroticism.* Rochester, NY: Inner
Traditions International, 1994.

Getty, Alice. *Ganesa.* New Delhi, India: Munshiram
Manoharlal, 1971.

Grimes, John A. *Ganapati: Song of the Self.*
Albany: State Univ. of New York P, 1995.

Hudson, Dennis. "The Ritual Worship of
Devi." in *Devi, The Great Goddess: Female
Divinity in South Asian Art,* by Vidya Dehejia,
page 91. Ahmedabad, India: Mapin Publishing, 1999.

O'Flaherty, Wendy Doniger. *Other People's
Myths.* Chicago: Univ. of Chicago P., 1995.

Subramaniyaswami, Satguru Sivaya.
*Dancing with Siva: Hinduism's Contemporary
Catechism.* Kauai, HI: Himalayan Academy. 1993.

ABOUT THE AUTHOR

James H. Bae is a practitioner of Hindu and Buddhist yoga and has trained as a monk in India. His areas of interest include Oriental medicine, Hindu and Buddhist art, and Eastern philosophy and culture. James is the author of *Darshan: Sweet Sounds of Surrender*, *In a World of Gods and Goddesses: The Mystic Art of Indra Sharma*, and *Smaranam: A Garland of Kirtan*, and a frequent writer for the Mandala deity minibooks. Bae was born in Harvey, Louisiana, and currently resides in Hilo, Hawaii.

MANDALA

P.O. Box 3088
San Rafael, CA 94912
www.mandalaearth.com

ISBN 978-1-68383-933-0

CEO: Raoul Goff
President: Kate Jerome
Publisher: Roger Shaw
Associate Publisher: Mariah Bear
Creative Director: Chrissy Kwasnik
Art Director: Allister Fein
Project Editor: Ian Cannon
2020 2021 2022 2023
10 9 8 7 6 5 4 3 2 1
Printed in China